Launching A Successful Affiliate Program Business

How To Start, Run, and Scale a Profitable Affiliate Program

HARRELL HOWARD

Table of Contents

Introduction	4
Part 1: Understanding the Basics of Affiliate Marketing	25
Chapter 1: What is Affiliate Marketing?	25
Chapter 2: The Benefits of an Affiliate Program	30
Chapter 3: Key Components of an Affiliate Program	34
Chapter 4: Legal and Ethical Considerations	39
Part 2: Starting Your Affiliate Program	45
Chapter 5: Planning Your Affiliate Program	45
Chapter 6: Choosing the Right Affiliate Model	49
Chapter 7: Selecting the Right Platform and Tools	54
Chapter 8: Setting Up Your Affiliate Program	62
Part 3: Running Your Affiliate Program	70
Chapter 9: Recruiting Affiliates	70
Chapter 10: Onboarding and Training Affiliates	78
Chapter 11: Affiliate Performance Tracking and Optimization	86
Chapter 12: Measuring and Reporting Success	94
Part 4: Advanced Strategies and Future Outlook	102
Chapter 13: International and Global Affiliate Marketing	102
Chapter 14: Emerging Trends and Future Outlook	110
Chapter 15: Affiliate Marketing in the Age of Privacy and Data Protection	121
Conclusion	129
Appendices	131
Templates and Checklists	**134**
• Affiliate Program Strategy Template	**134**
• Affiliate Recruitment Plan Template	**136**
• Affiliate Onboarding Checklist	**140**

- **Affiliate Performance Tracking Spreadsheet** 142
- **Affiliate Marketing Campaign Planning Template** 142
- **Influencer Outreach Email Template** 147
- **Affiliate Agreement Contract** 149

Introduction

Every day, businesses are constantly seeking innovative ways to expand their reach, drive sales, and forge lasting partnerships. Enter affiliate marketing - a dynamic and cost-effective strategy that has revolutionized the way companies approach online growth. This powerful marketing channel has emerged as a game-changer, offering unparalleled opportunities for businesses of all sizes to tap into new markets, boost their bottom line, and create mutually beneficial relationships with affiliates.

Imagine a world where your business can extend its influence far beyond its immediate sphere, reaching potential customers you never thought possible. Picture a marketing strategy that not only drives targeted traffic and sales but also aligns perfectly with your financial goals, ensuring you only pay for tangible results. This is the transformative power of affiliate marketing, and it's reshaping the way businesses approach their growth strategies in the digital age.

As we embark on this journey together, we'll explore the intricacies of launching, managing, and scaling a successful affiliate program. Whether you're a seasoned entrepreneur looking to diversify your marketing efforts or a business owner taking your first steps into the world of affiliate marketing, this book is designed to be your trusted companion and comprehensive guide.

Purpose of the Book

At its core, this book serves as a beacon of knowledge, illuminating the path to affiliate marketing success. Our primary aim is to equip you with a robust toolkit of practical strategies, insider insights, and proven techniques that will empower you to establish, nurture, and expand a thriving affiliate program.

Think of this book as your personal mentor in the world of affiliate marketing. We'll walk you through every step of the process, from the initial planning stages to the nuances of program management and the strategies for scaling your efforts. By the time you reach the final page, you'll have gained a wealth of knowledge that will transform you from a curious observer into a confident affiliate marketing strategist.

But this book isn't just about theoretical knowledge. We understand that in digital marketing, practical application is key. That's why we've packed these pages with actionable advice, real-world examples, and step-by-step guides that you can implement immediately in your business. Whether you're looking to launch your first affiliate program or optimize an existing one, you'll find the tools and strategies you need to succeed.

Why Affiliate Programs Are Powerful

The power of affiliate marketing lies in its unique ability to create symbiotic relationships between businesses and their affiliates. It's a marketing model that truly embodies the spirit of collaboration, where success for one party translates into success for the other.

Let's break down why affiliate programs have become such a formidable force in the digital marketing landscape:

1. **Expanded Reach and Brand Exposure:** Imagine having an army of brand ambassadors, each with their own loyal following, actively promoting your products or services. That's the reality of affiliate marketing. By partnering with affiliates, you're not just gaining additional marketing channels; you're tapping into established communities and audiences that

trust the affiliate's recommendations. This expanded reach can exponentially increase your brand's visibility and exposure, introducing your offerings to potential customers who might have never discovered you otherwise.

2. **Targeted Traffic and Qualified Leads:**

One of the most valuable aspects of affiliate marketing is its ability to drive highly targeted traffic to your business. Affiliates often specialize in specific niches or cater to particular demographics, allowing you to reach audiences that are already interested in products or services similar to yours. This targeted approach means that the traffic and leads generated through affiliate marketing are often more qualified and more likely to convert compared to broader marketing efforts.

3. **Performance-Based Model:**

Perhaps one of the most attractive features of affiliate marketing is its performance-based nature. Unlike traditional advertising methods where you pay upfront with no guarantee of results, affiliate marketing operates on a "pay for performance" model. This means you only compensate your affiliates when they generate tangible results - be it sales, leads, or other desired actions. This model significantly reduces the financial risk associated with marketing efforts and ensures that your marketing budget is directly tied to actual results.

4. **Cost-Effectiveness:**

The performance-based nature of affiliate marketing makes it an incredibly cost-effective strategy. By only paying for results, you're essentially outsourcing your sales efforts on a commission basis. This can be particularly beneficial for businesses with limited marketing budgets or those looking to optimize their marketing spend. Moreover, the initial setup costs for an affiliate program are often minimal compared to other marketing channels, making it an accessible option for businesses of all sizes.

5. **Scalability and Flexibility:**

   Affiliate programs offer unparalleled scalability. As your business grows, you can easily scale up your affiliate efforts by recruiting more affiliates or increasing commissions to incentivize higher performance. Conversely, if you need to scale back, you can adjust your program without the long-term commitments often associated with other marketing channels. This flexibility allows you to align your affiliate program with your business goals and market conditions, ensuring optimal performance at all times.

6. **Enhanced Credibility and Social Proof:**

   When affiliates promote your products or services, they're essentially vouching for your brand. This third-party endorsement can significantly enhance your credibility in the eyes of potential customers. In an era where consumers are increasingly skeptical of direct advertising, recommendations from trusted sources (like affiliates) can be incredibly powerful in influencing purchasing decisions.

7. **Access to Diverse Marketing Channels:** Affiliates come from various backgrounds and utilize different marketing channels. Some may be bloggers, others social media influencers, and some might specialize in email marketing or PPC advertising. By partnering with a diverse range of affiliates, you gain access to multiple marketing channels and strategies, effectively diversifying your marketing efforts without having to manage each channel directly.

8. **Data and Insights:** A well-managed affiliate program can provide valuable data and insights about your target audience. By analyzing which affiliates, channels, and promotions perform best, you

can gain a deeper understanding of your customers' preferences and behaviors. This information can inform not just your affiliate strategy, but your overall marketing and product development efforts.

9. **Long-Term Partnerships:**

Successful affiliate relationships often evolve into long-term partnerships. As affiliates become more familiar with your brand and products, and as they start seeing consistent returns from promoting your offerings, they're likely to become more invested in your success. These long-term relationships can lead to more stable, predictable revenue streams and opportunities for collaborative growth.

10. **Global Expansion Opportunities:**

Affiliate marketing can be an excellent way to test new markets or expand globally. By partnering with affiliates in different geographical locations, you can gain footholds in new markets without the significant upfront investment typically required for international expansion.

The power of affiliate marketing lies in its ability to create a win-win scenario for all parties involved. Businesses benefit from expanded reach, targeted traffic, and cost-effective marketing, while affiliates have the opportunity to monetize their platforms and provide value to their audiences. This mutually beneficial model has made affiliate marketing an indispensable component of many successful marketing strategies, driving growth and fostering valuable partnerships in the digital marketplace.

Who This Book Is For

This comprehensive guide is crafted with a diverse audience in mind, catering to individuals and businesses at various stages of their affiliate marketing journey. Whether you're a curious beginner or a seasoned professional looking to refine your strategies, this book has something valuable to offer. Let's explore who can benefit most from the insights shared in these pages:

1. **Entrepreneurs and Start-up Founders:**

   If you're an entrepreneur or start-up founder looking for cost-effective ways to grow your business and acquire customers, this book is your roadmap to leveraging affiliate marketing. You'll learn how to set up an affiliate program that aligns with your business goals and resources, allowing you to compete with larger players in your industry.

2. **E-commerce Store Owners:**

   For those running online stores, whether on platforms like Shopify, WooCommerce, or custom solutions, this book will show you how to harness the power of affiliate marketing to drive more traffic, increase sales, and build a network of promoters for your products.

3. **Digital Product Creators:**
If you're selling digital products such as e-books, courses, software, or subscription services, you'll discover strategies to expand your reach and increase sales through strategic affiliate partnerships.

4. **Marketing Professionals:**
Marketing managers, directors, and CMOs looking to diversify their marketing mix will find valuable insights on integrating affiliate marketing into their overall strategy. You'll learn how to measure the ROI of your affiliate efforts and optimize your campaigns for maximum impact.

5. **Affiliate Program Managers:**
For those already managing affiliate programs, this book offers advanced strategies to scale your efforts, improve affiliate relationships, and

drive better results. You'll gain insights into the latest trends and best practices in affiliate program management.

6. **Small Business Owners:**

   If you're a small business owner looking to compete in the digital space, this book will show you how affiliate marketing can level the playing field, allowing you to reach new customers without breaking the bank.

7. **Content Creators and Influencers:**

   While the focus is on businesses running affiliate programs, content creators and influencers will also find value in understanding how affiliate programs work from the merchant's perspective. This knowledge can help you become a more effective affiliate and build stronger partnerships with brands.

8. **Traditional Businesses Expanding Online:**

   For businesses with a traditional brick-and-mortar presence looking to expand their online footprint, this book will guide you through leveraging affiliate marketing as part of your digital transformation strategy.

9. **SaaS Companies:**

    Software-as-a-Service (SaaS) companies will learn how to structure affiliate programs that work well for subscription-based models, including strategies for reducing churn and maximizing customer lifetime value through affiliate partnerships.

10. **Affiliate Network Professionals:**

    Those working in affiliate networks or considering starting their own will gain insights into the needs and perspectives of both merchants and affiliates, helping you create more value for your clients.

11. **Students and Aspiring Digital Marketers:**

    If you're studying marketing or aspiring to build a career in digital marketing, this book will provide you with a solid foundation in affiliate marketing principles and practices, preparing you for real-world applications.

12. **Consultants and Agency Owners:** Marketing consultants and agency owners will find this book valuable in expanding their service offerings to include affiliate program management and strategy.

Regardless of your specific role or industry, if you have an online presence and are interested in exploring new avenues for growth and customer acquisition, this book is for you. The principles and strategies outlined here are adaptable to various business models and can be scaled to fit businesses of all sizes.

What Readers Will Learn

As you journey through the pages of this book, you'll embark on a comprehensive exploration of affiliate marketing, gaining insights and practical knowledge that will transform your approach to this powerful marketing channel. Here's a glimpse of what you can expect to learn:

1. Fundamental Concepts and Strategies:

- A deep dive into the core principles of affiliate marketing
- Understanding the affiliate marketing ecosystem and key players
- How to align affiliate marketing with your overall business strategy

2. Program Planning and Setup:

- Step-by-step guide to planning your affiliate program
- Choosing the right affiliate network or platform for your business
- Setting up tracking systems and commission structures

3. Affiliate Recruitment and Management:

- Strategies for identifying and recruiting high-quality affiliates
- Building and nurturing relationships with your affiliate partners
- Creating effective communication channels and support systems

4. Performance Tracking and Optimization:

- Implementing robust tracking mechanisms for accurate performance measurement
- Analyzing key metrics to assess program health and affiliate performance
- Techniques for continuous optimization and improvement of your program

5. Legal and Ethical Considerations:

- Navigating the legal landscape of affiliate marketing

- Understanding and implementing ethical practices
- Protecting your brand while fostering transparent affiliate relationships

6. Advanced Marketing Techniques:

- Leveraging content marketing in your affiliate strategy
- Harnessing the power of social media for affiliate promotion
- Implementing email marketing strategies for both merchant and affiliate success

7. Global Expansion Strategies:

- Adapting your affiliate program for international markets
- Overcoming challenges in cross-border affiliate marketing

- Localizing your approach for maximum global impact

8. Technology and Tools:

- Overview of essential tools and software for managing affiliate programs
- Integrating affiliate marketing with your existing tech stack
- Leveraging data and analytics for informed decision-making

9. Scaling Your Affiliate Program:

- Strategies for growing your affiliate network
- Balancing program expansion with quality control
- Adapting your program structure as your business grows

By the end of this book, you'll have gained not just theoretical knowledge, but practical skills and strategies that you can immediately apply to launch, manage, and scale a successful affiliate program. You'll be equipped with the tools to navigate the complexities of affiliate marketing, make data-driven decisions, and drive meaningful results for your business.

Whether you're looking to launch your first affiliate program or take your existing efforts to new heights, the comprehensive insights provided in this book will serve as your roadmap to success in the dynamic world of affiliate marketing.

As we move forward in this book, we'll dig deeper into how you can harness these benefits to create, manage, and scale a successful affiliate program for your business. We'll explore practical strategies, best practices, and real-world examples that will equip you with the knowledge and tools to thrive in the dynamic world of affiliate marketing.

Now, let's talk about Understanding the Basics of Affiliate Marketing and What is Affiliate Marketing in the next following chapter.

Part 1: Understanding the Basics of Affiliate Marketing

Chapter 1: What is Affiliate Marketing?

Definition and key concepts

Affiliate marketing is a performance-based marketing strategy in which businesses (known as merchants or advertisers) reward third-party publishers (known as affiliates) for driving traffic, leads, or sales to their products or services. Affiliates promote the merchant's offerings through various channels, such as websites, blogs, social media, and email marketing campaigns. When a consumer takes a desired action (e.g., making a purchase or submitting a lead form) through the affiliate's referral link or tracking code, the affiliate earns a commission.

This chapter will delve into the key concepts and terminology associated with affiliate marketing, ensuring that you have a solid foundation before diving deeper into the intricacies of launching and managing your own affiliate program.

Different types of affiliate programs

Affiliate programs can take various forms, depending on the goals and business model of the merchant. Some common types of affiliate programs include:

1. **Pay-per-sale (PPS)**: In this model, affiliates earn a commission based on actual sales they generate for the merchant. This is often a percentage of the sale value or a fixed amount per sale.
2. **Pay-per-lead (PPL)**: Affiliates are compensated for generating qualified leads, such as email signups or form submissions, rather than direct sales.

3. **Pay-per-click (PPC)**: Affiliates are paid a fixed amount for each click they generate to the merchant's website or landing page.
4. **Recurring revenue programs**: For businesses offering subscription-based products or services, affiliates can earn recurring commissions for each customer they refer who remains a paying subscriber.
5. **Two-tier programs**: In addition to earning commissions on direct referrals, affiliates can also earn a percentage of the commissions generated by sub-affiliates they recruit into the program.

Understanding the different types of affiliate programs will help you choose the most suitable model for your business goals and product offerings.

How affiliate marketing fits within the broader marketing strategy

Affiliate marketing should not be viewed as a standalone marketing strategy but rather as a complementary component of a broader, well-rounded marketing approach. By integrating affiliate marketing with other marketing channels, such as content marketing, email marketing, social media marketing, and paid advertising, businesses can create a powerful synergy that amplifies their reach, brand awareness, and overall marketing effectiveness.

For example, creating high-quality content can not only attract organic traffic and improve search engine rankings but also provide valuable resources for affiliates to promote and drive referrals. Similarly, email marketing campaigns can be leveraged to nurture existing customers and encourage them to join the affiliate program, while social media and influencer collaborations can tap into new audiences and drive targeted traffic.

By strategically aligning affiliate marketing with other marketing efforts, businesses can maximize their return on investment and create a holistic, cohesive marketing strategy that delivers long-term success.

Now that we are done talking about Understanding the Basics of Affiliate Marketing and What is Affiliate Marketing is, Let's talk about the benefits of an affiliate program in the next chapter.

Chapter 2: The Benefits of an Affiliate Program

Implementing an affiliate program can provide numerous benefits for businesses, making it a compelling addition to their overall marketing strategy. In this chapter, we will explore the key advantages of running an affiliate program and how it can contribute to the growth and success of your business.

Increased reach and sales

One of the most significant benefits of an affiliate program is its ability to extend your reach and drive more sales. By partnering with affiliates who have established audiences and influence, you can tap into new markets and potential customers that may have been difficult to reach through traditional marketing channels.

Affiliates act as brand ambassadors, promoting your products or services to their loyal followers and networks. This exposure can significantly increase your brand visibility, drive targeted traffic to your website, and ultimately result in more conversions and sales.

Moreover, the performance-based nature of affiliate marketing means that you only pay commissions when actual sales or desired actions are generated, aligning your marketing costs directly with revenue generation.

Cost-effectiveness

Compared to many traditional advertising methods, affiliate marketing can be highly cost-effective. Unlike upfront advertising costs, where you pay regardless of the results, affiliate marketing operates on a pay-for-performance model. This means that you only pay commissions to your affiliates when they generate actual sales or leads for your business.

By leveraging the efforts and reach of your affiliates, you can significantly reduce your marketing expenses while still achieving impressive results. This cost-effectiveness makes affiliate marketing an attractive option for businesses of all sizes, from startups with limited budgets to established enterprises looking to maximize their marketing ROI.

Building partnerships and relationships

Successful affiliate programs are built on strong partnerships and relationships between merchants and affiliates. By fostering these connections, businesses can cultivate a loyal network of affiliates who are invested in promoting their products or services.

Affiliates are motivated not only by the potential to earn commissions but also by the opportunity to align themselves with reputable brands and high-quality products or services. By treating affiliates as valued partners and providing them with the necessary resources, support, and incentives, businesses can foster long-lasting relationships that drive sustained success for both parties.

Furthermore, these partnerships can open doors to new opportunities, such as collaborative marketing campaigns, cross-promotions, and even product development or feedback loops. Building strong relationships with affiliates can lead to a mutually beneficial ecosystem that fuels growth and innovation for your business.

Now that we are done talking about the benefits of an affiliate program, Let's talk about the Key Components of an Affiliate Program in the next chapter.

Chapter 3: Key Components of an Affiliate Program

For an affiliate program to thrive, several key components must work in harmony. Understanding and effectively managing these components is crucial for ensuring the success of your affiliate marketing efforts. In this chapter, we will explore the essential elements that make up a well-structured affiliate program.

Merchants

As the business or brand offering products or services, merchants are at the core of an affiliate program. They are responsible for creating and managing the program, setting commission rates, providing marketing materials and resources to affiliates, and tracking and compensating affiliates for their referrals.

Merchants must clearly define their program terms, policies, and commission structures to ensure transparency and fairness for all involved parties. Additionally, they should strive to provide a compelling value proposition and attractive incentives to attract and retain high-performing affiliates.

Affiliates

Affiliates are the driving force behind an affiliate program's success. These individuals or businesses promote the merchant's products or services to their audiences, using various marketing channels such as websites, blogs, social media platforms, email lists, and more.

Successful affiliates often have a deep understanding of their target audience's interests and needs, allowing them to effectively promote relevant products or services. They leverage their influence, credibility, and marketing skills to drive targeted traffic and conversions for the merchant.

Merchants should strive to recruit and retain high-quality affiliates who align with their brand values and target market. Providing affiliates with the necessary resources, training, and support is crucial for fostering long-term, mutually beneficial partnerships.

Customers

Ultimately, the success of an affiliate program hinges on its ability to attract and convert customers. Customers are the end-users or consumers who make purchases or take desired actions based on the recommendations and promotions of affiliates.

Understanding customer behavior, preferences, and pain points is essential for crafting effective marketing campaigns and optimizing the customer journey. By providing a seamless and positive experience for customers, merchants can increase conversion rates, foster brand loyalty, and encourage repeat business.

Additionally, satisfied customers can become valuable advocates for the brand, further amplifying the reach and influence of the affiliate program through word-of-mouth and social proof.

Networks and platforms

While some merchants choose to run their affiliate programs in-house, many others leverage the services of affiliate networks or software platforms. These intermediaries provide a centralized platform for merchants to manage their affiliate programs, track performance, issue payments, and connect with a pool of potential affiliates.

Popular affiliate networks and platforms offer various features and tools to streamline the management of affiliate programs, such as real-time tracking, reporting, fraud detection, and automated commission calculations and payments.

Choosing the right affiliate network or platform can greatly simplify the administration of your affiliate program, allowing you to focus on strategy and growth while leveraging the expertise and resources provided by these specialized service providers.

Now that we are done talking about the Key Components of an Affiliate Program, Let's talk about the Legal and Ethical Considerations in the next chapter.

Chapter 4: Legal and Ethical Considerations

As with any business endeavor, it's crucial to understand and comply with the legal and ethical requirements surrounding affiliate marketing. This chapter will explore the key considerations and best practices to ensure your affiliate program operates within the bounds of the law and upholds ethical standards.

Compliance with regulations (e.g., FTC guidelines)

In many countries and regions, affiliate marketing activities are subject to various regulations and guidelines. One notable example is the Federal Trade Commission (FTC) guidelines in the United States, which require affiliates to disclose their relationships with merchants and ensure transparency in their endorsements and promotions.

Failure to comply with these regulations can result in significant penalties and legal consequences for both merchants and affiliates. It's essential to stay informed about the latest regulations and guidelines in the regions where your affiliate program operates and ensure that all parties involved are aware of and adhere to these requirements.

Ethical practices in affiliate marketing

Beyond legal compliance, it's crucial to uphold ethical practices in affiliate marketing to maintain trust, credibility, and long-term success. Some key ethical considerations include:

1. **Transparency**: Affiliates should be transparent about their relationships with merchants and disclose when they are promoting affiliate links or sponsored content.
2. **Authenticity**: Affiliates should only promote products or services they genuinely believe in

and have experience with, avoiding deceptive or misleading practices.

3. **Privacy and consent**: Merchants and affiliates must respect consumer privacy and obtain proper consent for data collection and marketing activities.

4. **Fair compensation**: Merchants should provide clear and fair compensation structures for affiliates, avoiding ambiguity or unfair treatment.

5. **Quality over quantity**: The focus should be on driving high-quality, relevant traffic and conversions rather than exploiting unethical tactics for short-term gains.

By fostering an ethical affiliate program culture, merchants can build trust with affiliates, customers, and the broader community, ultimately contributing to the long-term sustainability and success of their affiliate marketing efforts.

Privacy and data protection

We are in the digital age where privacy and data protection have become paramount concerns for businesses and consumers alike. Affiliate programs often involve the collection and processing of personal data, such as customer information, purchase histories, and affiliate tracking data.

Merchants and affiliates must ensure compliance with relevant data protection regulations, such as the General Data Protection Regulation (GDPR) in the European Union or the California Consumer Privacy Act (CCPA) in the United States. Failure to properly handle and protect personal data can result in severe penalties, reputational damage, and loss of consumer trust.

Best practices for privacy and data protection in affiliate marketing include:

1. Implementing robust data security measures to protect sensitive information from unauthorized access or breaches.
2. Obtaining explicit consent from consumers for data collection and usage, providing clear and transparent privacy policies.
3. Limiting data collection and retention to only what is necessary and relevant for the affiliate program's operations.
4. Ensuring that affiliates and third-party partners comply with data protection regulations and have appropriate safeguards in place.
5. Regularly reviewing and updating data protection policies and procedures to stay compliant with evolving regulations and industry best practices.

By prioritizing privacy and data protection, merchants can not only mitigate legal risks but also build trust and credibility with customers and partners, fostering a sustainable and ethical affiliate program ecosystem.

Now that we are done talking about the Legal and Ethical Considerations to look at in Affiliate program, Let's talk about starting and planning Your Affiliate Program in the next chapter.

Part 2: Starting Your Affiliate Program

Chapter 5: Planning Your Affiliate Program

Before diving into the implementation phase of your affiliate program, thorough planning and strategic considerations are crucial. This chapter will guide you through the essential steps of planning your affiliate program, ensuring a solid foundation for long-term success.

Setting goals and objectives

Clearly defined goals and objectives are the cornerstones of any successful affiliate program. Begin by identifying your primary motivations for launching an affiliate program, such as increasing brand awareness, driving sales, expanding into new markets, or acquiring new customers.

Once you have established your overarching goals, set specific, measurable, achievable, relevant, and time-bound (SMART) objectives. These objectives could include targets for revenue generation, customer acquisition, affiliate recruitment, or any other key performance indicators (KPIs) that align with your business priorities.

Having well-defined goals and objectives will not only guide your decision-making process but also provide a framework for measuring the success and effectiveness of your affiliate program over time.

Identifying your target audience

Understanding your target audience is essential for crafting an effective affiliate program strategy. Conduct market research to gain insights into the demographics, interests, pain points, and online behavior of your ideal customers. This information will inform the types of affiliates you should recruit, the promotional channels they should leverage, and the messaging and incentives that will resonate most effectively.

Additionally, analyze your existing customer base to identify potential brand advocates or influencers who could become valuable affiliates. Leveraging the power of word-of-mouth and social proof can significantly enhance the effectiveness of your affiliate program.

Researching the competition

Before launching your affiliate program, it's crucial to conduct a thorough competitive analysis. Identify key players in your industry or niche that have established affiliate programs and examine their strategies, commission structures, affiliate recruitment methods, and overall program offerings.

This research will help you identify potential opportunities, gaps in the market, and best practices that you can adapt or improve upon. By understanding the competitive landscape, you can differentiate your affiliate program and create a unique value proposition that attracts top-performing affiliates.

Additionally, monitoring your competitors' affiliate programs on an ongoing basis will enable you to stay ahead of industry trends, adjust your strategies as needed, and maintain a competitive edge in affiliate marketing.

Now that we are done talking about starting and planning Your Affiliate Program, Let's talk about Choosing the Right Affiliate Model in the next chapter.

Chapter 6: Choosing the Right Affiliate Model

Affiliate programs can operate under various commission models, each with its own advantages and considerations. In this chapter, we will explore the most common affiliate models and help you determine the best fit for your business goals and product offerings.

Pay-per-sale (PPS)

The pay-per-sale (PPS) model is one of the most widely used commission structures in affiliate marketing. Under this model, affiliates earn a commission, typically a percentage of the sale value or a fixed amount, for each successful sale they generate for the merchant.

The PPS model is particularly well-suited for e-commerce businesses, subscription-based services, and high-ticket product offerings. It aligns the incentives of affiliates with the merchant's primary goal of driving sales, making it an effective model for maximizing revenue generation.

However, it's important to strike the right balance with commission rates. Setting commissions too low may discourage affiliates from actively promoting your products, while excessively high commissions can eat into your profit margins. Conducting market research and analyzing industry standards can help you determine competitive and fair commission rates.

Pay-per-click (PPC)

In the pay-per-click (PPC) model, affiliates are compensated for each click they generate that leads to the merchant's website or landing page, regardless of whether a sale is made. This model is often used by merchants seeking to drive traffic and brand awareness, as well as those offering free or lead-generation products and services.

The PPC model can be advantageous for merchants looking to build their online presence and reach new audiences. However, it's important to carefully monitor and optimize conversion rates to ensure that the traffic generated by affiliates translates into desired actions and revenue.

Effective tracking and fraud prevention measures are crucial in PPC affiliate programs, as affiliates may be incentivized to generate clicks through unethical means, such as automated bots or click farms.

Pay-per-lead (PPL)

The pay-per-lead (PPL) model rewards affiliates for generating qualified leads, such as email signups, form submissions, or trial registrations. This model is commonly used by businesses offering free trials, software-as-a-service (SaaS) products, or services that require lead nurturing and sales follow-up.

The PPL model allows merchants to leverage the reach and influence of affiliates to build their lead pipeline and potentially convert those leads into paying customers over time. However, it's essential to clearly define what constitutes a qualified lead and to have robust lead tracking and management systems in place.

Effective lead scoring and nurturing strategies are critical for maximizing the value of affiliate-generated leads and ensuring a positive return on investment (ROI) for the affiliate program.

Hybrid models

While the PPS, PPC, and PPL models are the most common, some merchants may choose to implement hybrid models that combine elements of two or more commission structures. For example, a merchant could offer a small PPC commission to incentivize affiliates to drive traffic, combined with a higher PPS commission for actual sales generated.

Hybrid models can be tailored to specific business needs and product offerings, providing flexibility and incentives for affiliates to engage in various desired actions. However, they can also introduce additional complexity in tracking, reporting, and commission calculations, requiring robust affiliate management systems and processes.

Now that we are done talking about Choosing the Right Affiliate Model, Let's talk about Selecting the Right Platform and Tools in the next chapter.

Chapter 7: Selecting the Right Platform and Tools

Choosing the right affiliate platform and tools is crucial for the efficient management and success of your affiliate program. This chapter will guide you through the process of evaluating and selecting the most suitable platform and tools to meet your specific needs.

Overview of popular affiliate networks and software

There are numerous affiliate networks and software platforms available in the market, each offering a range of features and capabilities. Some popular options include:

1. **Affiliate networks**: These are third-party platforms that connect merchants with a pool of potential affiliates. Examples include

ShareASale, Rakuten Advertising (formerly LinkShare), Commission Junction (CJ), and Awin.

2. **Self-hosted affiliate software**: These are software solutions that merchants can install and host on their own servers, providing greater control and customization options. Examples include Post Affiliate Pro, iDevAffiliate, and Scaleo.

3. **Cloud-based affiliate software**: These are software-as-a-service (SaaS) solutions hosted in the cloud, offering scalability and accessibility without the need for in-house hosting. Examples include Refersion, LeadDyno, and Tapfiliate.

4. **Plugins and extensions**: For merchants using popular e-commerce platforms like Shopify, WooCommerce, or Magento, there are various affiliate plugins and extensions available that

can integrate seamlessly with their existing systems.

When evaluating these options, it's important to consider factors such as ease of use, feature set, scalability, pricing, and integration capabilities with your existing tech stack.

Criteria for choosing the right platform

Selecting the right affiliate platform is a critical decision that can significantly impact the success and efficiency of your affiliate program. Here are some key criteria to consider:

1. **Features and functionality**: Evaluate the features offered by each platform and ensure they align with your specific requirements, such as tracking capabilities, commission management, reporting and analytics, fraud detection, and affiliate management tools.

2. **Scalability**: As your affiliate program grows, the platform should be able to accommodate increasing traffic, affiliates, and transactions without compromising performance or functionality.
3. **Ease of use**: Both merchants and affiliates should find the platform user-friendly and intuitive, minimizing the learning curve and ensuring efficient onboarding and management.
4. **Integration capabilities**: Assess the platform's ability to integrate seamlessly with your existing systems, such as e-commerce platforms, Customer Relationship Management (CRM) software, and analytics tools.
5. **Support and resources**: Consider the level of support and resources provided by the platform, such as documentation, training materials, and customer service responsiveness.

6. **Pricing and fees**: Evaluate the pricing structure, including any setup fees, monthly or annual subscriptions, and transaction fees, to ensure it aligns with your budget and provides a favorable return on investment (ROI).

7. **Security and compliance**: Ensure the platform adheres to industry standards and regulations for data security, privacy, and compliance, particularly when handling sensitive information like customer data and financial transactions.

By carefully evaluating these criteria, you can select a platform that not only meets your current needs but also has the flexibility and scalability to support your affiliate program's future growth and evolution.

Tools for tracking and managing affiliates

In addition to selecting the right affiliate platform, there are several complementary tools and technologies that can enhance the tracking, management, and optimization of your affiliate program:

1. **Link tracking and attribution**: Tools like Voluum, RedTrack, and HasOffers allow you to create and track unique affiliate links, attribute conversions accurately, and prevent fraud.
2. **Analytics and reporting**: Platforms like Google Analytics, Mixpanel, and Heap provide in-depth insights into user behavior, conversion rates, and affiliate performance, enabling data-driven decision-making.
3. **Content Distribution Networks (CDNs)**: Using CDNs like Cloudflare or Amazon CloudFront can improve the speed and performance of your affiliate marketing assets, such as banners, videos, and landing pages, leading to better user experiences and higher conversion rates.

4. **Affiliate management and communication:** Customer Relationship Management (CRM) tools like Hubspot or Zoho can streamline affiliate communication, onboarding, and relationship management.

5. **Payment and commission processing:** Integrating with payment gateways and solutions like PayPal, Stripe, or Tipalti can simplify the process of issuing affiliate commissions and payments.

6. **Fraud detection and prevention:** Implementing tools like FraudScore, MaxMind, or Sift can help identify and mitigate fraudulent affiliate activity, protecting your program's integrity and profitability.

By leveraging these complementary tools and technologies, you can optimize various aspects of your affiliate program, from tracking and attribution to analytics, communication, and fraud prevention, ultimately driving better performance and results.

Now that we are done talking about Selecting the Right Platform and Tools , Let's talk about Setting Up Your Affiliate Program in the next chapter.

Chapter 8: Setting Up Your Affiliate Program

With the planning and platform selection phases complete, it's time to dive into the practical steps of setting up your affiliate program. This chapter will guide you through the process of creating program terms and conditions, determining commission structures, and designing marketing materials and resources for affiliates.

Creating program terms and conditions

Clearly defined program terms and conditions are essential for establishing a fair and transparent framework for your affiliate program. These terms should outline the expectations, rules, and regulations that govern the relationships between merchants and affiliates.

Some key elements to include in your program terms and conditions are:

1. **Eligibility criteria**: Specify the requirements for becoming an affiliate, such as having a relevant website or audience, meeting minimum traffic thresholds, or adhering to specific content guidelines.
2. **Commission structure**: Clearly define the commission rates, payment schedules, and any qualifying criteria for earning commissions.
3. **Cookie tracking and attribution**: Explain how affiliate referrals will be tracked, including cookie duration, attribution models, and any exceptions or limitations.
4. **Promotion guidelines**: Outline the acceptable and prohibited methods for promoting your products or services, such as restricting the use of certain advertising channels or ensuring compliance with advertising regulations.
5. **Termination and suspension policies**: Specify the conditions under which an affiliate

account may be terminated or suspended, such as violations of program terms, fraudulent activities, or extended periods of inactivity.

6. **Intellectual property rights**: Clarify the ownership and permitted use of trademarks, logos, and other branding assets provided to affiliates for promotional purposes.

7. **Data privacy and security**: Ensure compliance with relevant data privacy regulations and outline the responsibilities of affiliates in handling customer data securely.

8. **Dispute resolution**: Establish a clear process for resolving disputes or disagreements between merchants and affiliates.

By creating comprehensive and legally sound program terms and conditions, you can establish clear expectations, minimize misunderstandings, and protect the interests of both your business and your affiliate partners.

Setting commission structures and incentives

Determining an appropriate commission structure and incentive program is crucial for attracting and retaining high-performing affiliates. While commission rates can vary widely across industries and product categories, it's essential to strike a balance between offering competitive incentives and maintaining profitability.

Here are some factors to consider when setting commission structures:

1. **Industry standards**: Research the commission rates offered by competitors in your industry or niche to ensure your rates are competitive and attractive to affiliates.
2. **Product margins**: Analyze your product margins and pricing to determine the maximum commission rates you can afford while maintaining profitability.

3. **Performance tiers**: Consider implementing tiered commission structures that reward top-performing affiliates with higher commission rates based on predefined performance thresholds.

4. **Recurring revenue commissions**: For subscription-based products or services, offer recurring commissions to incentivize affiliates to promote your offerings and encourage customer retention.

5. **Bonus and incentive programs**: Implement bonus programs, contests, or other incentives to motivate affiliates and drive specific behaviors or promotional activities.

6. **Payment schedules**: Clearly communicate payment schedules, such as monthly, quarterly, or upon reaching a minimum earnings threshold, to manage affiliate expectations and cash flow.

Regularly reviewing and optimizing your commission structures and incentive programs can help you stay competitive, attract and retain top talent, and maximize the return on investment (ROI) of your affiliate program.

Designing marketing materials and resources for affiliates

Providing affiliates with high-quality marketing materials and resources is essential for enabling them to effectively promote your products or services. These assets should not only be visually appealing and on-brand but also informative and persuasive, helping affiliates communicate the value proposition and benefits to their audiences.

Some key marketing materials and resources to consider include:

1. **Creative assets**: Banners, logos, product images, and videos that affiliates can use on

their websites, social media platforms, or other marketing channels.

2. **Promotional materials**: Sales copy, email swipe copies, social media post templates, and other pre-written promotional content that affiliates can easily repurpose and customize.

3. **Product information and training**: Comprehensive product descriptions, features, benefits, and training materials to ensure affiliates have a deep understanding of your offerings.

4. **Brand guidelines**: Provide clear branding guidelines outlining acceptable logo usage, color palettes, and other visual identity elements to maintain brand consistency.

5. **Affiliate onboarding and resource hub**: Create a centralized hub or portal where affiliates can access all relevant materials, program updates, and support resources.

6. **Affiliate tracking and reporting tools:** Provide affiliates with access to tracking and reporting tools to monitor their performance, earnings, and commission payouts.

By equipping affiliates with high-quality marketing materials and resources, you empower them to effectively promote your products or services, increasing their chances of success and driving better results for your affiliate program.

Now that we are done talking about Setting Up Your Affiliate Program, Let's talk about Running Your Affiliate Program and Recruiting Affiliates in the next chapter.

Part 3: Running Your Affiliate Program

Chapter 9: Recruiting Affiliates

With your affiliate program set up and marketing materials ready, the next critical step is to actively recruit and onboard high-quality affiliates. This chapter will explore strategies for identifying potential affiliates, creating an appealing affiliate offer, and conducting effective outreach campaigns.

Identifying potential affiliates

The success of your affiliate program hinges on attracting the right affiliates who can effectively promote your products or services to their audiences. Here are some strategies for identifying potential affiliate partners:

1. **Industry research:** Conduct research to identify influencers, bloggers, content creators,

and websites within your industry or niche that align with your target audience.

2. **Competitor analysis**: Examine the affiliate networks and programs used by your competitors and identify top-performing affiliates who may be interested in joining your program.

3. **Customer analysis**: Look within your existing customer base for brand advocates, loyal customers, or influential individuals who could make valuable affiliate partners.

4. **Social media monitoring**: Monitor social media platforms, forums, and online communities related to your industry to identify influential voices and potential affiliate candidates.

5. **Affiliate marketplaces**: Leverage affiliate marketplaces and directories, such as ShareASale, Rakuten Advertising, or CJ

Affiliate, to search for and connect with affiliates relevant to your niche.

6. **Referral programs**: Implement a referral program that incentivizes your existing affiliates to recruit new affiliates, leveraging their networks and connections.

By identifying and targeting the right affiliates, you increase the likelihood of attracting partners who can effectively promote your products or services and drive meaningful results for your affiliate program.

Outreach strategies

Once you have identified potential affiliate partners, it's crucial to develop effective outreach strategies to capture their interest and secure their participation in your program. Here are some best practices for successful affiliate outreach:

1. **Personalized approach**: Craft personalized outreach messages that demonstrate your

understanding of the affiliate's audience, niche, and unique value proposition, rather than using generic templates.

2. **Value proposition**: Clearly communicate the benefits and incentives of joining your affiliate program, such as competitive commission rates, marketing materials, and support resources.

3. **Success stories and social proof**: Share success stories, case studies, or testimonials from existing affiliates to demonstrate the potential for earning and the quality of your program.

4. **Multi-channel outreach**: Consider using a combination of channels for outreach, such as email, social media, forums, or direct messaging, to increase visibility and engagement.

5. **Follow-up and persistence**: Be prepared to follow up with potential affiliates multiple

times, as it may take several touchpoints to secure their interest and commitment.

6. **Referral incentives**: Offer incentives or bonuses for successful referrals from existing affiliates, leveraging their networks and relationships.

By implementing a strategic and personalized outreach approach, you can effectively communicate the value of your affiliate program and increase the likelihood of attracting high-quality affiliates who can drive meaningful results for your business.

Creating an appealing affiliate offer

To attract and retain top-performing affiliates, it's essential to craft an appealing and competitive affiliate offer that stands out in the market. Here are some key elements to consider when developing your affiliate offer:

1. **Competitive commission rates**: Research industry standards and offer commission rates that are attractive and aligned with the value your affiliates can provide.

2. **Recurring revenue opportunities**: For subscription-based or recurring revenue models, offer ongoing commissions or residual payments to incentivize affiliates to promote customer retention.

3. **Exclusive promotions and discounts**: Provide affiliates with exclusive promotional offers, discounts, or bonus incentives that they can leverage to increase conversions and stand out from competitors.

4. **Marketing and promotional resources**: Equip affiliates with high-quality marketing materials, creative assets, and promotional resources to support their efforts and increase their chances of success.

5. **Dedicated affiliate support**: Offer dedicated support channels, account managers, or resources to assist affiliates with onboarding, training, and ongoing program-related inquiries.

6. **Affiliate contests and incentives**: Implement contests, leaderboards, or special incentives to motivate and reward top-performing affiliates, fostering healthy competition and encouraging higher engagement.

7. **Affiliate community and networking opportunities**: Create opportunities for affiliates to connect, collaborate, and share best practices, fostering a sense of community and facilitating peer-to-peer learning.

By crafting an attractive and comprehensive affiliate offer that addresses the needs and motivations of top-performing affiliates, you can differentiate your program and increase your chances of recruiting and retaining high-quality partners.

Now that we are done talking about Running Your Affiliate Program and Recruiting Affiliates, Let's talk about Onboarding and Training Affiliates in the next chapter.

Chapter 10: Onboarding and Training Affiliates

Effective onboarding and training are essential for setting your affiliates up for success and ensuring they have the knowledge and resources necessary to effectively promote your products or services. This chapter will explore best practices for creating comprehensive welcome kits, providing training programs and webinars, and offering continuous support and communication.

Welcome kits and resources

A well-designed welcome kit can set the tone for a positive and productive relationship with your new affiliates. Consider including the following elements in your welcome kit:

1. **Program overview and guidelines:** Provide a concise overview of your affiliate program,

including key terms and conditions, commission structures, and promotional guidelines.

2. **Getting started guide:** Offer a step-by-step guide to help affiliates set up their accounts, integrate tracking codes, and access essential resources.

3. **Creative assets and promotional materials:** Supply affiliates with a range of creative assets, such as banners, product images, videos, and pre-written promotional copy, to assist them in their marketing efforts.

4. **Performance tracking and reporting:** Explain how affiliates can access real-time performance data, track their commissions, and generate customized reports.

5. **Training and educational resources:** Provide access to training videos, webinars, or written tutorials that cover best practices, promotional

strategies, and tips for maximizing their success within your program.

6. **Communication channels and support:** Clearly outline the available communication channels, such as a dedicated affiliate manager, email support, or online forums, to ensure affiliates can easily ask questions and receive timely assistance.

7. **Branding guidelines:** Share your brand guidelines, including logos, color palettes, and messaging guidelines, to help affiliates create consistent and on-brand promotional content.

8. **Success stories and case studies:** Highlight success stories and case studies from top-performing affiliates, showcasing the potential for growth and success within your program.

By providing a comprehensive and well-designed welcome kit, you can set the stage for a smooth onboarding experience, foster engagement, and equip affiliates with the necessary resources to hit the ground running and achieve success within your program.

Training programs and webinars

In addition to providing comprehensive welcome kits, offering ongoing training programs and webinars can help ensure affiliates have the knowledge and skills necessary to succeed in promoting your products or services effectively.

1. **Onboarding training**: Conduct live or pre-recorded onboarding training sessions to walk affiliates through the basics of your program, best practices for promotion, and an overview of available marketing materials and resources.
2. **Product training**: Provide in-depth product training to help affiliates gain a thorough

understanding of your offerings, features, benefits, and unique selling points, enabling them to communicate effectively with their audiences.

3. **Marketing and promotion training**: Offer training on effective marketing and promotion strategies, such as content marketing, social media marketing, email marketing, and other relevant tactics for their specific niches or audiences.

4. **Success stories and case studies**: Share success stories and case studies of top-performing affiliates, highlighting their strategies, tactics, and best practices for driving results.

5. **Webinars and Q&A sessions**: Host regular webinars or live Q&A sessions to address common questions, share program updates, and provide opportunities for affiliates to interact and learn from each other.

By investing in comprehensive training programs and resources, you can empower affiliates with the knowledge and skills they need to effectively promote your products or services, ultimately leading to better performance and higher returns for your affiliate program.

Ongoing support and communication

Providing continuous support and maintaining open lines of communication with your affiliates is crucial for fostering long-term success and engagement. Consider implementing the following strategies:

1. **Dedicated support channels**: Offer dedicated support channels such as email, live chat, or a support ticketing system specifically for affiliates, ensuring their inquiries and concerns are addressed promptly and efficiently.
2. **Account management**: Assign dedicated account managers or program coordinators to

high-performing affiliates, providing personalized support, guidance, and assistance in optimizing their promotional efforts.

3. **Affiliate newsletter or updates**: Regularly communicate program updates, new promotional opportunities, success stories, and other relevant information through a dedicated affiliate newsletter or email updates.

4. **Affiliate community forums or groups**: Create online communities or forums where affiliates can connect, collaborate, share best practices, and engage with your program team and fellow affiliates.

5. **Affiliate performance reporting**: Provide affiliates with access to real-time performance reporting and analytics, enabling them to track their progress, identify areas for improvement, and make data-driven decisions.

6. **Feedback and suggestions**: Actively solicit feedback and suggestions from affiliates, using

their insights to continuously improve your program, offerings, and support resources.

By prioritizing ongoing support, communication, and fostering a sense of community among your affiliates, you can maintain high levels of engagement, loyalty, and motivation, ultimately driving better performance and results for your affiliate program.

Now that we are done talking about Onboarding and Training Affiliates, Let's talk about Affiliate Performance Tracking and Optimization in the next chapter.

Chapter 11: Affiliate Performance Tracking and Optimization

Monitoring and optimizing affiliate performance is crucial for maximizing the return on investment (ROI) of your affiliate program. This chapter will explore strategies for tracking and analyzing affiliate performance metrics, identifying top performers, and implementing optimization techniques to drive better results.

Tracking and analyzing performance metrics

To effectively monitor and optimize your affiliate program, it's essential to track and analyze key performance metrics. Here are some important metrics to consider:

1. **Affiliate sales and revenue**: Track the total sales and revenue generated by each affiliate, allowing you to identify top-performing

partners and assess their overall contribution to your program.

2. **Conversion rates**: Monitor conversion rates by affiliate, enabling you to identify affiliates who are driving high-quality traffic and conversions, as well as those who may need additional support or optimization.

3. **Commission payouts**: Track commission payouts to affiliates to ensure accurate and timely payments, as well as to analyze the return on investment (ROI) of your affiliate program.

4. **Traffic sources and referral channels**: Analyze the traffic sources and referral channels used by affiliates to identify the most effective marketing channels and promotion strategies.

5. **Customer acquisition costs**: Calculate the customer acquisition costs associated with each affiliate to assess the profitability and efficiency of their promotional efforts.

6. **Customer lifetime value**: Track the lifetime value of customers acquired through affiliates to identify partners who drive high-value, long-term customers.

By regularly analyzing these performance metrics, you can gain valuable insights into the effectiveness of your affiliate program and make data-driven decisions to optimize and refine your strategies.

Identifying and leveraging top-performing affiliates

Within your affiliate program, there will likely be a subset of top-performing affiliates who drive a disproportionate amount of sales and revenue. Identifying and leveraging these high-performers can be a valuable strategy for maximizing the impact of your affiliate program.

1. **Analyze performance data**: Regularly review and analyze performance data to identify your

top-performing affiliates based on metrics such as sales, revenue, conversion rates, and customer lifetime value.

2. **Offer incentives and exclusive opportunities**: Provide top-performing affiliates with exclusive incentives, bonus commissions, or early access to new products or promotions to incentivize and reward their continued high performance.

3. **Seek feedback and insights**: Engage with your top affiliates to gather feedback, insights, and best practices that can be shared with other affiliates or used to refine your overall program strategies.

4. **Leverage success stories and case studies**: Highlight the success stories and case studies of your top-performing affiliates, using them as inspiration and motivation for other affiliates to emulate their strategies and tactics.

5. **Foster a sense of community and exclusivity**: Create a sense of community and exclusivity among your top-performing affiliates, fostering a sense of belonging and encouraging them to continue their exceptional performance.

By identifying and leveraging your top-performing affiliates, you can concentrate your efforts on the partners driving the most significant impact, while also using their insights and success stories to inspire and motivate other affiliates in your program.

Optimization strategies and techniques

Continuous optimization is key to maximizing the effectiveness and profitability of your affiliate program. Here are some strategies and techniques to consider:

1. **A/B testing**: Conduct A/B tests on various elements of your affiliate program, such as

commission structures, marketing materials, landing pages, or promotional strategies, to identify and implement the most effective approaches.

2. **Affiliate segmentation and targeting**: Segment your affiliates based on factors such as niche, audience demographics, marketing channels, or performance levels, and tailor your strategies, resources, and support to meet the specific needs of each segment.

3. **Commission rate adjustments**: Regularly review and adjust commission rates based on performance data, industry trends, and competitive benchmarks to ensure you are offering competitive incentives while maintaining profitability.

4. **Marketing and promotional strategy refinement**: Continuously refine your marketing and promotional strategies based on performance data, affiliate feedback, and

emerging trends, ensuring your affiliates have access to the most effective tactics and resources.

5. **Fraud prevention and monitoring**: Implement robust fraud prevention and monitoring measures to identify and mitigate any fraudulent or unethical activities within your affiliate program, protecting your brand reputation and revenue.

6. **Program rules and guidelines updates**: Regularly review and update your program rules and guidelines to address new challenges, industry regulations, or changes in best practices, ensuring your program remains compliant and aligned with evolving standards.

By embracing a culture of continuous optimization and data-driven decision-making, you can consistently refine and improve the performance of your affiliate program, maximizing its impact on your business goals and driving sustainable, long-term success.

Now that we are done talking about Affiliate Performance Tracking and Optimization, Let's talk about Measuring and Reporting Success in the next chapter.

Chapter 12: Measuring and Reporting Success

Accurately measuring and reporting the success of your affiliate program is essential for demonstrating its value, identifying areas for improvement, and making informed decisions about its future direction. This chapter will explore key performance indicators (KPIs), data analysis techniques, and best practices for reporting and communicating program results to stakeholders.

Defining key performance indicators (KPIs)

To effectively measure the success of your affiliate program, it's crucial to define and track relevant key performance indicators (KPIs). Here are some common KPIs to consider:

1. **Affiliate program revenue**: Track the total revenue generated by your affiliate program,

including sales, subscriptions, and recurring revenue streams.

2. **Return on investment (ROI)**: Calculate the return on investment (ROI) of your affiliate program by comparing the revenue generated to the costs associated with running the program, such as commission payouts, software fees, and marketing expenses.

3. **Conversion rates**: Monitor conversion rates at various stages of the customer journey, such as click-through rates, lead-to-sale conversion rates, and customer retention rates.

4. **Customer acquisition cost (CAC)**: Calculate the customer acquisition cost (CAC) through your affiliate program to assess its efficiency and profitability compared to other marketing channels.

5. **Customer lifetime value (CLV)**: Measure the customer lifetime value (CLV) of customers acquired through your affiliate program to

evaluate the long-term impact and profitability of this acquisition channel.

6. **Affiliate program growth**: Track the growth of your affiliate program over time, including the number of active affiliates, new affiliate signups, and overall program participation and engagement.

By defining and regularly monitoring these KPIs, you can gain a comprehensive understanding of the performance and impact of your affiliate program, enabling data-driven decision-making and continuous optimization.

Data analysis and reporting techniques

Effective data analysis and reporting are essential for deriving actionable insights from your affiliate program data and communicating its success to stakeholders. Consider implementing the following techniques:

1. **Data visualization tools**: Utilize data visualization tools, such as dashboards, charts, and graphs, to present complex data in a clear and visually appealing manner, making it easier to identify trends and patterns.
2. **Segmentation and cohort analysis**: Segment your data by various factors, such as affiliate performance levels, marketing channels, or customer demographics, to uncover valuable insights and tailor your strategies accordingly.
3. **Attribution modeling**: Implement attribution modeling techniques to accurately attribute revenue and conversions to specific affiliates, marketing channels, or touchpoints along the customer journey.
4. **Predictive analytics**: Leverage predictive analytics techniques, such as machine learning algorithms, to forecast future performance, identify potential risks or opportunities, and optimize your affiliate program strategies.

5. **Benchmark analysis**: Compare your affiliate program performance against industry benchmarks, competitors, or historical data to gain perspective on its relative success and identify areas for improvement.

6. **Automated reporting and scheduling**: Implement automated reporting and scheduling tools to ensure consistent and timely delivery of performance reports to relevant stakeholders, minimizing manual effort and improving efficiency.

By leveraging these data analysis and reporting techniques, you can derive meaningful insights from your affiliate program data and effectively communicate its impact and value to stakeholders, enabling informed decision-making and continuous program optimization.

Communicating results and success stories

Effective communication of your affiliate program's results and success stories is crucial for maintaining stakeholder buy-in, motivating affiliates, and demonstrating the value of your efforts. Consider the following strategies:

1. **Executive summaries and dashboards**: Develop concise executive summaries and visually appealing dashboards to present key performance metrics, highlights, and success stories to senior leadership and stakeholders.

2. **Affiliate success stories and case studies**: Highlight the achievements and best practices of your top-performing affiliates through success stories and case studies, sharing valuable insights and inspiring other affiliates to emulate their strategies.

3. **Affiliate newsletters and updates**: Regularly communicate program updates, performance highlights, and success stories to your affiliate

base through dedicated newsletters or email campaigns, fostering engagement and motivation.

4. **Social media and content marketing**: Leverage social media channels and content marketing tactics, such as blog posts or videos, to share your affiliate program's success stories and achievements with a wider audience.

5. **Internal communication and recognition**: Celebrate the successes of your affiliate program within your organization by sharing updates and recognizing the contributions of team members involved in its management and growth.

6. **Industry events and conferences**: Participate in relevant industry events and conferences to showcase your affiliate program's success, share best practices, and network with potential affiliates and partners.

By effectively communicating your affiliate program's results and success stories, you can maintain stakeholder buy-in, motivate and inspire your affiliates, and position your program as a leader in the industry, ultimately driving continued growth and success.

Now that we are done talking about Measuring and Reporting Success, Let's talk about Advanced Strategies and Future Outlook and International and Global Affiliate Marketing in the next chapter.

Part 4: Advanced Strategies and Future Outlook

Chapter 13: International and Global Affiliate Marketing

As businesses increasingly operate in a globalized market, expanding your affiliate program to reach international audiences presents both opportunities and challenges. This chapter will explore strategies for adapting your affiliate program to different markets, navigating cultural and regulatory nuances, and leveraging global affiliate networks.

Adapting your program for different markets

Successful international expansion requires adapting your affiliate program to the unique characteristics and preferences of each target market. Here are some key considerations:

1. **Cultural nuances**: Understand and respect cultural differences in communication styles, design preferences, and consumer behavior, tailoring your marketing materials, messaging, and strategies accordingly.
2. **Language and localization**: Offer localized versions of your website, marketing materials, and affiliate resources in the native languages of your target markets, ensuring effective communication and engagement.
3. **Payment and commission structures**: Research and adapt your commission structures and payment methods to align with local preferences, regulations, and business practices in each market.
4. **Legal and regulatory compliance**: Ensure compliance with local laws and regulations related to advertising, data privacy, intellectual property, and other relevant areas, seeking legal counsel as needed.

5. **Competitor analysis**: Conduct thorough competitor analysis in each target market to understand the competitive landscape, identify potential affiliate partners, and develop differentiated strategies.
6. **Local partnerships and affiliates**: Establish partnerships with local influencers, content creators, and affiliates who have a deep understanding of the market and can effectively promote your products or services.

By thoughtfully adapting your affiliate program to the unique nuances of each target market, you can increase your chances of success, build a strong local presence, and maximize the potential of your international expansion efforts.

Navigating cultural and regulatory nuances

Expanding your affiliate program globally requires navigating a complex landscape of cultural and regulatory nuances. Here are some key considerations:

1. **Cultural sensitivity**: Develop a deep understanding of cultural norms, values, and sensitivities in each target market, ensuring your marketing materials, messaging, and promotional strategies are respectful and resonate with local audiences.

2. **Advertising regulations**: Familiarize yourself with local advertising regulations, including restrictions on certain products or services, data privacy laws, and guidelines for endorsements or sponsored content.

3. **Intellectual property protection**: Understand and comply with local intellectual property laws and regulations, ensuring proper usage and protection of your trademarks, copyrights, and other intellectual property assets.

4. **Tax and financial regulations**: Research and comply with tax laws, financial regulations, and reporting requirements related to affiliate commissions and payments in each market.

5. **Language and translation considerations**: Ensure accurate and culturally appropriate translation of marketing materials, legal agreements, and affiliate resources, leveraging professional translation services or local expertise when necessary.

6. **Local partnerships and advisors**: Consider partnering with local agencies, consultants, or legal advisors who can provide valuable insights, guidance, and support in navigating the unique cultural and regulatory landscapes of each market.

By proactively addressing these nuances and seeking expert guidance when needed, you can mitigate risks, build trust and credibility with local audiences, and position your affiliate program for long-term success in international markets.

Leveraging global affiliate networks

While establishing direct relationships with local affiliates is valuable, leveraging global affiliate networks can also provide access to a diverse pool of international affiliates and streamline your program management. Here are some key considerations:

1. **Global affiliate network selection**: Research and evaluate global affiliate networks that have a strong presence and affiliate base in your target markets, considering factors such as reputation, affiliate quality, technology capabilities, and support services.
2. **Integration and implementation**: Integrate your affiliate program with the chosen global network(s), ensuring proper setup, tracking, and

commission management across multiple markets and currencies.

3. **Affiliate recruitment and management:** Leverage the affiliate recruitment tools and resources provided by the global networks, while also actively seeking out and nurturing direct relationships with high-performing international affiliates.

4. **Localization and cultural adaptation:** Collaborate with the global networks to ensure proper localization and cultural adaptation of your affiliate program materials and resources for each target market.

5. **Performance tracking and optimization:** Utilize the analytics and reporting capabilities of the global networks to track and optimize the performance of your international affiliate program, identifying top-performing markets and affiliates.

6. **Compliance and regulatory support:** Leverage the expertise and guidance of the global networks in navigating local compliance and regulatory requirements, minimizing risks and ensuring adherence to local laws and best practices.

By effectively leveraging global affiliate networks, in conjunction with direct affiliate relationships and local partnerships, you can expand your reach, tap into diverse international audiences, and streamline the management of your global affiliate program.

Now that we are done talking about Advanced Strategies and Future Outlook and International and Global Affiliate Marketing, Let's talk about Emerging Trends and Future Outlook in the next chapter.

Chapter 14: Emerging Trends and Future Outlook

The affiliate marketing landscape is constantly evolving, driven by technological advancements, changing consumer behaviors, and shifting market dynamics. This chapter will explore emerging trends and provide insights into the future outlook of affiliate marketing, helping you stay ahead of the curve and position your program for long-term success.

Influencer marketing and brand ambassadors

Influencer marketing has become a powerful force in the digital marketing landscape, and its integration with affiliate marketing presents exciting opportunities. Here are some key considerations:

1. **Influencer identification and partnerships:** Identify and partner with relevant influencers and brand ambassadors who align with your

brand values and target audience, leveraging their reach and influence to promote your products or services.

2. **Influencer compensation models**: Explore various compensation models, such as commission-based, flat-fee, or hybrid structures, to incentivize influencers and align their interests with your business goals.

3. **Content collaborations and campaigns**: Collaborate with influencers on content creation, social media campaigns, product reviews, and sponsored posts, leveraging their authentic voices and trusted relationships with their audiences.

4. **Performance tracking and attribution**: Implement robust tracking and attribution mechanisms to accurately measure the impact of influencer partnerships on sales, leads, and other key performance indicators (KPIs).

5. **Disclosure and transparency**: Ensure compliance with relevant laws and regulations regarding influencer marketing, such as disclosure requirements for sponsored content and endorsements.

6. **Long-term relationship building**: Foster long-term relationships with top-performing influencers and brand ambassadors, providing them with exclusive opportunities, incentives, and support to maintain their engagement and advocacy for your brand.

By effectively integrating influencer marketing into your affiliate program, you can leverage the power of social proof, authenticity, and engaged audiences to drive brand awareness, credibility, and conversions.

Automation and artificial intelligence

The integration of automation and artificial intelligence (AI) technologies is transforming various aspects of affiliate marketing, enabling more efficient processes, personalized experiences, and data-driven decision-making. Here are some potential applications:

1. **Affiliate recruitment and onboarding**: Utilize AI-powered chatbots and intelligent matching algorithms to streamline affiliate recruitment, onboarding, and matching processes, ensuring a seamless and personalized experience for new affiliates.

2. **Performance optimization and fraud detection**: Leverage machine learning algorithms and predictive analytics to optimize affiliate performance, identify high-potential partners, and detect fraudulent activities or compliance violations.

3. **Content generation and personalization**: Implement AI-powered content generation and personalization tools to create tailored

marketing materials, product descriptions, and promotional assets for affiliates, ensuring relevance and effectiveness for their specific audiences.

4. **Customer segmentation and targeting**: Utilize AI-driven customer segmentation and targeting techniques to identify high-value customer segments and match them with the most suitable affiliates or influencers for personalized promotion.

5. **Chatbots and virtual assistants**: Integrate chatbots and virtual assistants powered by natural language processing (NLP) to provide real-time support, answer common questions, and assist affiliates with program navigation and optimization.

6. **Predictive analytics and forecasting**: Leverage predictive analytics and forecasting models to anticipate trends, identify emerging opportunities, and make data-driven decisions

about program strategies, commission structures, and resource allocation.

By embracing automation and AI technologies, you can streamline processes, enhance personalization, and gain valuable insights, positioning your affiliate program for greater efficiency, effectiveness, and competitive advantage.

Emerging marketing channels and technologies

The digital marketing landscape is constantly evolving, with new channels and technologies emerging regularly. Staying ahead of these trends can provide opportunities for innovative affiliate marketing strategies. Here are some potential areas to explore:

1. **Voice and conversational marketing**: Optimize your affiliate program and marketing materials for voice search and conversational interfaces, such as smart speakers and virtual

assistants, to reach consumers in new and engaging ways.

2. **Augmented reality (AR) and virtual reality (VR)**: Leverage AR and VR technologies to create immersive product experiences, virtual showrooms, and interactive promotional campaigns for affiliates to share with their audiences.

3. **Metaverse and Web3 integration**: Explore opportunities within emerging virtual worlds and decentralized platforms, such as the metaverse and Web3 ecosystems, to establish affiliate partnerships and create unique brand experiences.

4. **Livestreaming and shoppable videos**: Integrate livestreaming and shoppable video capabilities into your affiliate program, enabling affiliates to showcase products, conduct live demonstrations, and facilitate real-time purchases.

5. **Innovative ad formats and platforms**: Stay informed about emerging ad formats and platforms, such as interactive ads, playable ads, and social commerce integrations, and explore their potential for affiliate marketing campaigns.

6. **Internet of Things (IoT) and connected devices**: As IoT devices become more prevalent, consider ways to integrate affiliate marketing strategies into connected home appliances, wearables, and other smart devices.

By actively monitoring and embracing emerging marketing channels and technologies, you can position your affiliate program as an innovative and forward-thinking leader, reaching new audiences and delivering engaging and immersive experiences.

Sustainability and ethical considerations

As consumers become increasingly conscious of environmental and social issues, incorporating sustainability and ethical practices into your affiliate program can resonate with socially responsible audiences and align with broader corporate values. Here are some key considerations:

1. **Sustainable and eco-friendly products and services**: Partner with affiliates who promote sustainable, eco-friendly, or socially responsible products and services, aligning your program with conscious consumerism trends.
2. **Ethical marketing practices**: Implement ethical marketing guidelines and standards for your affiliate program, ensuring transparency, truthful advertising, and respect for consumer privacy and data protection.
3. **Diversity and inclusion initiatives**: Foster a diverse and inclusive affiliate base, actively seeking partnerships with underrepresented groups and creating opportunities for diverse voices and perspectives.

4. **Charitable initiatives and cause marketing**: Explore partnerships with non-profit organizations or cause-related marketing campaigns, allowing affiliates to promote and support social or environmental causes aligned with your brand values.

5. **Carbon offsetting and environmental initiatives**: Implement carbon offsetting programs or support environmental initiatives to mitigate the carbon footprint of your affiliate program and promote sustainability efforts.

6. **Ethical supply chain and labor practices**: Ensure your affiliate program partners and suppliers adhere to ethical labor practices, fair trade principles, and responsible sourcing standards throughout the supply chain.

By incorporating sustainability and ethical considerations into your affiliate program, you can build trust and credibility with conscious consumers, attract socially responsible affiliates, and contribute to a more sustainable and equitable future.

Now that we are done talking about Emerging Trends and Future Outlook, Let's talk about Affiliate Marketing in the Age of Privacy and Data Protection in the next chapter.

Chapter 15: Affiliate Marketing in the Age of Privacy and Data Protection

As data privacy and protection regulations continue to evolve, it is crucial for affiliate marketers to adapt their practices and ensure compliance. This chapter will explore strategies for navigating the changing privacy landscape, protecting consumer data, and maintaining transparency and trust within your affiliate program.

Data privacy regulations and compliance

Staying up-to-date with data privacy regulations and ensuring compliance is essential for maintaining the integrity and longevity of your affiliate program. Here are some key considerations:

1. **GDPR and other data protection laws**: Understand and comply with the General Data Protection Regulation (GDPR) and other

relevant data protection laws in the regions where you operate, ensuring proper handling and protection of personal data.

2. **Cookie consent and tracking transparency**: Implement cookie consent mechanisms and provide clear disclosure about data tracking practices, allowing consumers to make informed choices about their privacy preferences.

3. **Data security and breach prevention**: Implement robust data security measures, such as encryption, access controls, and breach prevention protocols, to protect consumer data from unauthorized access or misuse.

4. **Third-party vendor and affiliate compliance**: Ensure that third-party vendors, affiliates, and partners involved in your program adhere to your data privacy and security standards, providing appropriate training and contractual obligations.

5. **Privacy impact assessments**: Conduct regular privacy impact assessments to identify potential risks, vulnerabilities, and areas for improvement in your data handling practices.
6. **Staying informed and adapting to changes**: Monitor changes in data privacy regulations and industry best practices, and be prepared to adapt your policies, procedures, and technology solutions accordingly.

By prioritizing data privacy and compliance, you can build trust with consumers, mitigate legal and reputational risks, and position your affiliate program as a responsible and trustworthy partner in the evolving privacy landscape.

Transparency and consumer trust

Maintaining transparency and fostering consumer trust are critical components of a successful affiliate marketing program in the age of data privacy. Here are some strategies to consider:

1. **Clear and accessible privacy policies**: Develop clear and easy-to-understand privacy policies that outline your data collection, usage, and sharing practices, ensuring consumers can make informed decisions.

2. **Opt-in and consent mechanisms**: Implement opt-in and consent mechanisms for data collection and usage, respecting consumer preferences and giving them control over their personal information.

3. **Affiliate disclosure and transparency**: Require affiliates to disclose their relationship with your brand and any sponsored or affiliate content, adhering to relevant advertising regulations and industry guidelines.

4. **Data privacy education and awareness**: Provide educational resources and awareness

campaigns to help consumers understand data privacy rights, best practices, and the steps you're taking to protect their information.

5. **Grievance and feedback mechanisms**: Establish accessible grievance and feedback mechanisms for consumers to report concerns, request data access or deletion, or provide input on your privacy practices.

6. **Third-party audits and certifications**: Consider undergoing third-party audits or obtaining certifications related to data privacy and security, demonstrating your commitment to best practices and accountability.

By prioritizing transparency, consumer education, and trust-building initiatives, you can differentiate your affiliate program as a responsible and ethical player in the industry, fostering long-term loyalty and advocacy among consumers and affiliates alike.

Data minimization and ethical use of data

In addition to compliance and transparency, it's essential to adopt a mindset of data minimization and ethical use of data within your affiliate program. Here are some key principles to consider:

1. **Data minimization**: Collect and retain only the minimum amount of personal data necessary to fulfill the legitimate purposes of your affiliate program, minimizing potential risks and liabilities.
2. **Purpose limitation**: Use personal data solely for the purposes specified and communicated to consumers, avoiding secondary or unrelated uses without explicit consent.
3. **Data anonymization and pseudonymization**: Implement data anonymization and pseudonymization techniques to protect consumer privacy while still enabling data analysis and insights.

4. **Ethical data processing and algorithms**: Ensure that data processing algorithms and decision-making models used within your affiliate program are free from biases, discrimination, and unintended consequences that could harm consumers.

5. **Data retention and deletion policies**: Establish clear data retention and deletion policies, regularly purging or anonymizing personal data that is no longer necessary for legitimate business purposes.

6. **Ethical data sharing and monetization**: If sharing or monetizing consumer data with third parties, ensure transparency, obtain explicit consent, and prioritize ethical data practices that respect consumer privacy and rights.

By embracing data minimization and ethical data use principles, you can demonstrate your commitment to responsible data stewardship, build trust with consumers and affiliates, and mitigate potential legal and reputational risks associated with data mishandling or misuse.

Conclusion

Affiliate marketing continues to evolve and present exciting opportunities for businesses to expand their reach, drive revenue, and foster long-lasting partnerships. By implementing the strategies outlined in this comprehensive guide, you can build a robust and successful affiliate program that delivers tangible results while maintaining transparency, trust, and ethical practices.

Remember, affiliate marketing is not a one-size-fits-all approach. Continuously adapt and tailor your strategies to align with changing consumer behaviors, emerging technologies, and industry trends. Embrace innovation, leverage data and insights, and prioritize sustainability and ethical considerations to future-proof your affiliate program.

Success in affiliate marketing hinges on fostering strong relationships with affiliates, influencers, and partners. Invest in their growth, provide exceptional support, and create a sense of community built on shared values and mutual success. Celebrate achievements, learn from challenges, and continuously optimize your program to stay ahead of the curve.

As you embark on this exciting journey, remember that affiliate marketing is not just a transactional endeavor but an opportunity to build lasting connections, drive meaningful impact, and contribute to a more sustainable and ethical digital landscape.

Embrace the power of affiliate marketing, stay agile, and unleash the full potential of your brand and partnerships. The future is bright, and the opportunities are endless for those who embrace innovation, collaboration, and a commitment to excellence.

Appendices

Glossary of Terms

Affiliate: An individual or entity that promotes a company's products or services in exchange for a commission on any resulting sales or leads.

Affiliate Marketing: A performance-based marketing strategy where affiliates earn commissions for promoting a company's products or services and driving sales or leads.

Affiliate Network: A platform or intermediary that connects merchants (advertisers) with affiliates, manages tracking, reporting, and payment processes.

Affiliate Program: The structured program set up by a merchant to recruit, manage, and compensate affiliates for promoting their products or services.

Commission Rate: The percentage or fixed amount paid to affiliates for each successful sale or lead generated through their promotional efforts.

Conversion Rate: The percentage of visitors or leads that complete a desired action, such as making a purchase or filling out a form.

Cookie: A small data file stored on a user's device by a website, used for tracking and identifying users across multiple sessions.

Cost per Action (CPA): An affiliate marketing pricing model where affiliates are paid for each specific action taken by a visitor or lead, such as a sale, lead form submission, or subscription.

Influencer Marketing: A form of marketing that involves partnering with individuals (influencers) who have a significant online following and credibility within a specific niche or industry.

Landing Page: A standalone web page designed specifically for a marketing or advertising campaign, often used to capture leads or drive conversions.

Pay per Click (PPC): An affiliate marketing pricing model where affiliates are paid a fixed amount for each click that they generate to the merchant's website or landing page.

Publisher: Another term for an affiliate, referring to the individual or entity that publishes or promotes a merchant's products or services.

Sub-affiliate: An affiliate who is recruited and managed by another affiliate, forming a multi-tier affiliate network.

Tracking and Attribution: The process of monitoring and crediting affiliate referrals, sales, and commissions to the appropriate affiliates using tracking technologies and attribution models.

Templates and Checklists

• Affiliate Program Strategy Template

1. Program Objectives

Define your primary goals for the affiliate program:

> e.g., Increase sales by 20%, Expand market reach, Boost brand awareness

2. Target Audience

Describe your ideal affiliate partners:

> e.g., Niche bloggers, Social media influencers, Industry experts

3. Commission Structure

Outline your commission model:

- Commission Type (e.g., Pay-per-sale, Pay-per-lead)
- Commission Rate (e.g., 10% of sale, $50 per lead)
- Payment Threshold (e.g., $100 minimum payout)

4. Affiliate Tools and Resources

List the resources you'll provide to affiliates:

> e.g., Banners, Text links, Product feeds, Marketing materials

5. Tracking and Reporting

Describe your tracking and reporting system:

> Tracking Method (e.g., Cookies, Unique coupon codes)

> Cookie Duration (e.g., 30 days)

> Reporting Frequency (e.g., Real-time, Daily, Weekly)

6. Affiliate Recruitment Strategy

Outline your plan to attract and onboard affiliates:

> e.g., Outreach emails, Social media campaigns, Affiliate networks

7. Performance Metrics

List the key performance indicators (KPIs) you'll track:

e.g., Conversion rate, Average order value, Click-through rate, Return on ad spend (ROAS)

8. Compliance and Terms

Summarize key points of your affiliate agreement:

e.g., Prohibited promotional methods, Intellectual property guidelines, Commission reversals policy

9. Program Management

Describe how you'll manage the program:

Program Manager (e.g., In-house team, Outsourced agency)

Affiliate Communication (e.g., Monthly newsletter, Dedicated support email)

Performance Reviews (e.g., Quarterly affiliate evaluations)

10. Budget and ROI Projections

Outline your financial expectations:

Program Setup Costs

Projected Monthly Commission Payout

Expected ROI (e.g., 300% within first year)

- **Affiliate Recruitment Plan Template**

1. Ideal Affiliate Profile

Describe your ideal affiliate partner:

> e.g., Niche, audience size, content type, engagement rates

2. Value Proposition

What makes your affiliate program attractive?

> e.g., Competitive commission rates, exclusive products, strong brand reputation

3. Recruitment Channels

List the channels you'll use to find and approach potential affiliates:

Channel	Strategy
e.g., Social Media	e.g., LinkedIn outreach, Instagram DMs
e.g., Affiliate Networks	e.g., Join relevant networks, create compelling program listings
e.g., Email Outreach	e.g., Personalized emails to industry bloggers

4. Outreach Message Template

Draft a template for your initial outreach message:

> Subject: Exciting Partnership Opportunity with [Your Brand]
>
> Dear [Affiliate Name],
>
> I hope this email finds you well. I'm reaching out because we've been impressed with your content in the [specific niche] space and believe there could be a great opportunity for us to collaborate...

5. Onboarding Process

Outline the steps for onboarding new affiliates:

1. [e.g., Application review]
2. [e.g., Welcome email with program details]
3. [e.g., Provide access to affiliate dashboard]
4. [e.g., Initial training call or webinar]
5. [e.g., Share marketing materials and resources]

6. Recruitment Goals

Set specific, measurable goals for your recruitment efforts:

| Short-term goal (e.g., Recruit 20 affiliates in the first month) |
| Medium-term goal (e.g., Reach 100 active affiliates within 6 months) |
| Long-term goal (e.g., Build a network of 500+ affiliates by end of year) |

7. Incentives for Early Adopters

List any special incentives for affiliates who join early:

```
e.g., Higher commission rates for first 3 months, exclusive product access, feature on your website
```

8. Performance Tracking

How will you measure the success of your recruitment efforts?

```
e.g., Number of applications received, conversion rate from outreach to sign-up, quality of recruited affiliates (based on performance metrics)
```

9. Timeline and Milestones

Create a timeline for your recruitment campaign:

Date	Milestone
e.g., Week 1	e.g., Finalize outreach materials
e.g., Week 2-4	e.g., Initial outreach campaign
e.g., Month 2	e.g., Review and optimize strategy

10. Budget Allocation

Outline the budget for your recruitment efforts:

- Total recruitment budget
- Allocation for paid promotions (e.g., sponsored posts, ads)
- Allocation for incentives and bonuses
- Allocation for tools and resources (e.g., outreach software)

• Affiliate Onboarding Checklist

1. Initial Contact and Welcome

- ☐ Send welcome email
- ☐ Schedule welcome call or video chat
- ☐ Provide program overview and expectations

Ensure the affiliate feels valued and understands the next steps.

2. Account Setup

- ☐ Create affiliate account in your system
- ☐ Send login credentials
- ☐ Verify affiliate's contact and payment details

Double-check all information for accuracy to avoid future issues.

3. Program Training

- ☐ Provide product/service training
- ☐ Explain commission structure and payment terms
- ☐ Review promotional guidelines and best practices
- ☐ Conduct compliance and legal requirements training

Ensure the affiliate fully understands how to promote effectively and compliantly.

4. Resource Provision

- ☐ Share marketing materials (banners, text links, etc.)
- ☐ Provide content creation guidelines
- ☐ Explain how to generate and use tracking links
- ☐ Give access to FAQ and knowledge base

Equip the affiliate with all necessary tools for success.

5. Communication Channels

- ☐ Provide affiliate support contact information
- ☐ Add to affiliate newsletter list
- ☐ Invite to affiliate community or forum (if applicable)

Ensure the affiliate knows how to get help and stay informed.

6. Performance Tracking

- ☐ Provide tutorial on using the affiliate dashboard
- ☐ Explain available reporting and analytics tools
- ☐ Review key performance indicators (KPIs)

Help the affiliate understand how to track and improve their performance.

7. First Campaign Support

- ☐ Assist with planning first promotional campaign
- ☐ Review and approve initial promotional content
- ☐ Provide support during campaign launch

Offer hands-on support to ensure a successful start.

8. Follow-up and Feedback

- ☐ Schedule follow-up call after first week
- ☐ Send onboarding experience feedback survey
- ☐ Set date for first performance review

Gather insights to improve the onboarding process and address any concerns.

- **Affiliate Performance Tracking Spreadsheet**

Affiliate Performance Tracking Spreadsheet

Affiliate ID	Name	Clicks	Conversions	Conversion Rate	Total Sales	Commission	EPC	Status
AFF001	John Doe	1500	75	5.00%	$7,500	$750	$0.50	Active
AFF002	Jane Smith	2000	60	3.00%	$6,000	$600	$0.30	Active
AFF003	Bob Johnson	800	16	2.00%	$1,600	$160	$0.20	Probation
AFF004	Sarah Williams	3000	150	5.00%	$15,000	$1,500	$0.50	Active
AFF005	Mike Brown	1200	42	3.50%	$4,200	$420	$0.35	Active

- **Affiliate Marketing Campaign Planning Template**

1. Campaign Overview

Campaign Name:

Campaign Objective:

Start Date:
dd / mm / yyyy

End Date:
dd / mm / yyyy

Target Audience:

2. Product/Service Details

Product/Service Name:

Product/Service Description:

Unique Selling Points:

Pricing:

3. Affiliate Details

Commission Structure:

Affiliate Requirements:

Resources Provided to Affiliates:

4. Marketing Channels

Social Media Platforms:

Content Marketing Strategies:

Email Marketing Plans:

Paid Advertising Channels:

5. Creative Assets

Banner Ads:

Text Links:

Landing Pages:

Email Templates:

6. Tracking and Reporting

Tracking Method:

Key Performance Metrics:

Reporting Frequency:

Daily

7. Compliance and Legal

Disclosure Requirements:

Prohibited Practices:

Content Approval Process:

8. Budget

Total Campaign Budget:

Commission Budget:

Marketing Materials Budget:

Additional Expenses:

9. Timeline and Milestones

Key Dates and Milestones:

10. Evaluation and Optimization

Success Criteria:

Optimization Strategies:

- Influencer Outreach Email Template

Subject: Collaboration Opportunity with [Your Brand Name]

Dear [Influencer's Name],

I hope this email finds you well. My name is [Your Name], and I'm reaching out from [Your Company/Brand Name]. We've been following your work on [Social Media Platform] and are impressed by your [specific aspect of their content, e.g., fashion sense, travel adventures, cooking skills].

> I particularly enjoyed your recent post about [mention a specific post or content they created]. Your authentic approach to [relevant topic] resonates with our brand values.

We believe there could be an exciting opportunity for us to collaborate. [Your Company/Brand Name] specializes in [brief description of your product/service], and we think your audience would be interested in what we have to offer.

Here's what we had in mind:

- [Collaboration idea 1, e.g., Sponsored post featuring our product]
- [Collaboration idea 2, e.g., Instagram story takeover]
- [Collaboration idea 3, e.g., Exclusive discount code for your followers]

We're open to your ideas and would love to hear your thoughts on how we can create engaging content together that adds value to your audience.

If you're interested, we'd be happy to discuss the details further, including compensation and deliverables. We're flexible and aim to create a partnership that's mutually beneficial.

Thank you for your time, [Influencer's Name]. We look forward to the possibility of working together.

Best regards,

[Your Name]
[Your Position]
[Your Company/Brand Name]
[Your Contact Information]

- Affiliate Agreement Contract

This Affiliate Agreement (the "Agreement") is made and entered into as of [Date] , by and between:

Company: [Company Name] , with its principal place of business located at [Company Address] (hereinafter referred to as the "Company")

and

Affiliate: [Affiliate Name] , with its principal place of business located at [Affiliate Address] (hereinafter referred to as the "Affiliate")

1. Appointment of Affiliate

The Company hereby appoints the Affiliate as a non-exclusive affiliate to promote and market the Company's products or services in accordance with the terms and conditions set forth in this Agreement.

2. Responsibilities of Affiliate

The Affiliate agrees to:

1. Use its best efforts to promote and market the Company's products or services.
2. Comply with all applicable laws, regulations, and the Company's policies and guidelines.
3. Not engage in any deceptive, misleading, or unethical practices.
4. Not make any representations or warranties concerning the Company's products or services beyond those expressly authorized by the Company.
5. Use only marketing materials and product descriptions provided or approved by the Company.

3. Commission Structure

The Company agrees to pay the Affiliate a commission of [Commission Percentage] % on all qualifying sales generated through the Affiliate's unique tracking link. Qualifying sales are defined as [Definition of Qualifying Sales] .

4. Payment Terms

Commissions will be calculated on a [monthly/quarterly] basis and paid within [Number of Days] days after the end of each [month/quarter] . The minimum payout threshold is [Minimum Payout Amount] .

5. Term and Termination

This Agreement shall commence on the date first written above and shall continue until terminated by either party with [Notice Period] days written notice. The Company reserves the right to terminate this Agreement immediately if the Affiliate breaches any term of this Agreement.

6. Intellectual Property

The Affiliate acknowledges that all trademarks, logos, and other intellectual property related to the Company's products or services are the sole property of the Company. The Affiliate is granted a limited, non-exclusive license to use these materials solely for the purpose of promoting the Company's products or services under this Agreement.

7. Confidentiality

The Affiliate agrees to maintain the confidentiality of any proprietary information disclosed by the Company during the course of this Agreement and for a period of [Time Period] after its termination.

8. Indemnification

The Affiliate agrees to indemnify and hold harmless the Company from any claims, damages, or expenses arising from the Affiliate's breach of this Agreement or any misrepresentation made by the Affiliate.

9. Governing Law

This Agreement shall be governed by and construed in accordance with the laws of [State/Country].

10. Entire Agreement

This Agreement constitutes the entire understanding between the parties with respect to the subject matter hereof and supersedes all prior agreements, oral or written, made between the parties relating to the subject matter hereof.

IN WITNESS WHEREOF, the parties hereto have executed this Agreement as of the date first above written.

_____   _____

For the Company   For the Affiliate

Name: [Company Representative Name]   Name: [Affiliate Representative Name]

ABOUT THE AUTHOR

Harrell Howard is a prolific author and thought leader, specializing in a diverse array of subjects that cater to both personal and professional development. With a deep passion for empowering readers through knowledge, Harrell has penned numerous best-selling books, each offering practical insights and actionable strategies across various fields.

Harrell Howard combines a rich background in technology, marketing, and personal development to deliver content that is both insightful and practical.

When he's not writing, Harrell enjoys exploring new tech, market trends, and sharing his knowledge via speaking engagements and workshops. His drive for lifelong learning & passion for helping others is evident in his book.

www.ingramcontent.com/pod-product-compliance
Lightning Source LLC
Chambersburg PA
CBHW071925210526
45479CB00002B/558